ANIMAL BATTLES

MANED WOLF VS. GIANT ANTEATER

BY NATHAN SOMMER

TORQUE, AN IMPRINT OF BELLWETHER MEDIA BY FLUTTERBEE

Torque brims with excitement perfect for thrill-seekers of all kinds. Discover daring survival skills, explore uncharted worlds, and marvel at mighty engines and extreme sports. In *Torque* books, anything can happen. Are you ready?

This edition first published in 2026 by Bellwether Media, Inc.

For information regarding permission, write to Bellwether Media, Inc., Attention: Permissions Department, 3500 American Blvd W, Suite 150, Bloomington, MN 55431.

Library of Congress Cataloging-in-Publication Data is available at www.loc.gov or upon request from the publisher.

9798893048353 (hardcover)
9798898800154 (paperback)
9798893049350 (ebook)

Editor: Suzane Nguyen   Designer: Josh Brink   Series Designer: Andrea Schneider

Printed in the United States of America, North Mankato, MN.

TABLE OF CONTENTS

THE COMPETITORS 4
SECRET WEAPONS 10
ATTACK MOVES 16
READY, FIGHT! 20
GLOSSARY 22
TO LEARN MORE 23
INDEX 24

THE COMPETITORS

South America's grasslands are home to many **predators**. Maned wolves have **adapted** to these **habitats**. They use their height to take smaller **prey** by surprise.

Maned wolves share these habitats with giant anteaters. These **mammals** use sharp claws to stand up to enemies. Who wins when these two animals come face-to-face?

KNUCKLE WALKERS

Giant anteaters walk on their knuckles to keep their long claws safe.

MANED WOLF PROFILE

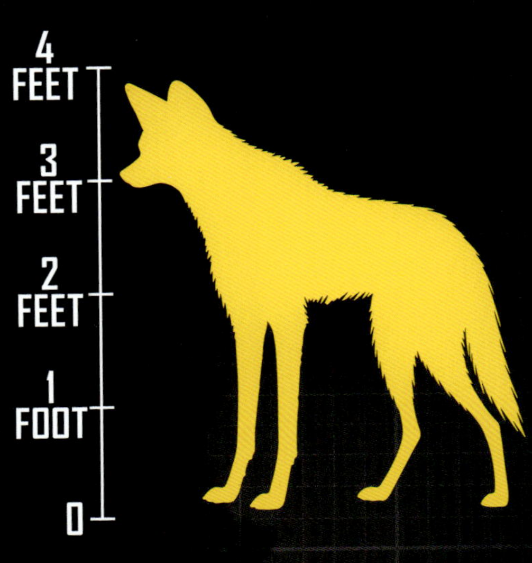

WEIGHT

AROUND 50 POUNDS (23 KILOGRAMS)

HEIGHT

UP TO 3 FEET (1 METER) AT THE SHOULDER

HABITATS

FORESTS

GRASSLANDS

SAVANNAS

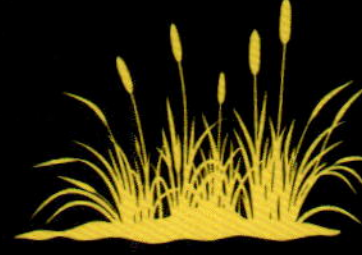
WETLANDS

MANED WOLF RANGE

Maned wolves are South America's largest **canines**. They stand up to 3 feet (1 meter) tall at the shoulder. They weigh around 50 pounds (23 kilograms). Maned wolves have thick red fur and long black legs. Large, pointed ears sit atop their heads.

Maned wolves are found in central and eastern South America. They prefer grasslands and forests.

BEHIND THE NAME

Maned wolves are named after the dark fur on their neck and shoulders.

Giant anteaters are the world's largest anteaters. They grow up to 8 feet (2.4 meters) long. They weigh up to 140 pounds (63.5 kilograms). Giant anteaters have gray fur with black and white stripes and bushy tails. Their long **snouts** have no teeth.

The mammals live in South and Central America. They prefer grasslands, **wetlands**, and forests.

SUPERPOWER SMELL

Giant anteaters have a sense of smell 40 times stronger than a human's.

GIANT ANTEATER PROFILE

LENGTH

UP TO 8 FEET (2.4 METERS)

WEIGHT

UP TO 140 POUNDS (63.5 KILOGRAMS)

HABITATS

WETLANDS

GRASSLANDS

FORESTS

GIANT ANTEATER RANGE

SECRET WEAPONS

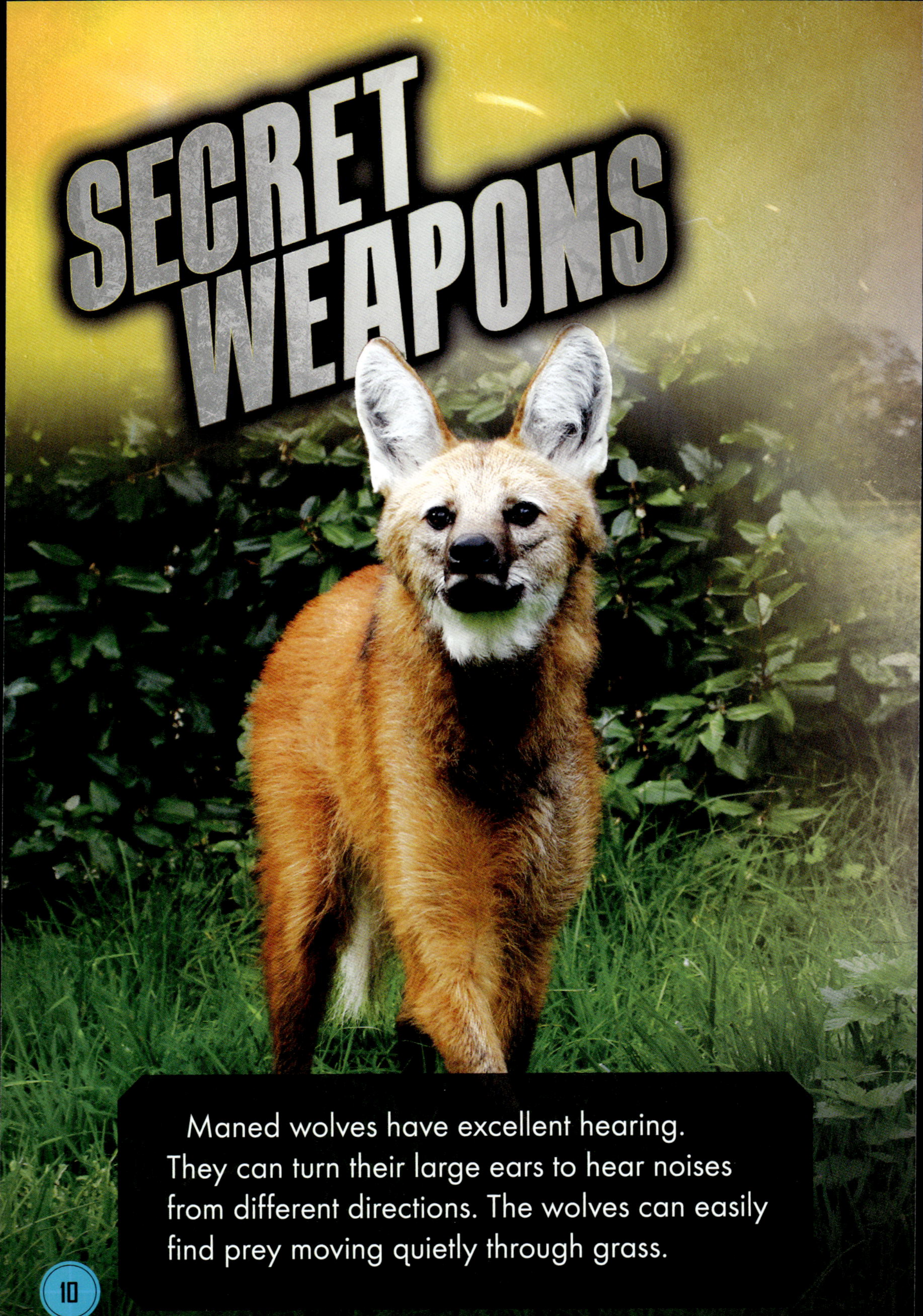

Maned wolves have excellent hearing. They can turn their large ears to hear noises from different directions. The wolves can easily find prey moving quietly through grass.

Giant anteaters use their powerful noses to help them find food. They can sniff out different kinds of **insect** mounds. They can even smell insects underground.

Maned wolves use their long legs and speed to catch prey and escape predators in tall grasses. The wolves can run up to 30 miles (48 kilometers) per hour.

Giant anteaters have long, sharp front claws. These allow them to tear into thick insect mounds. They also use their claws as weapons to cut enemies.

EXCELLENT HEARING

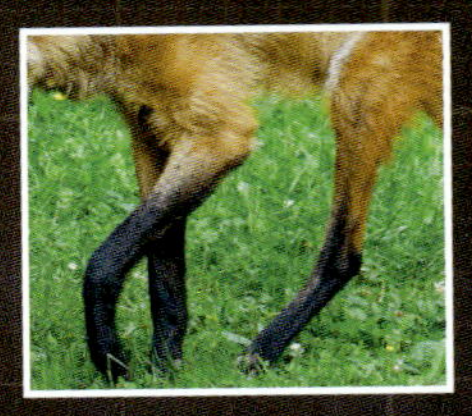

LONG LEGS

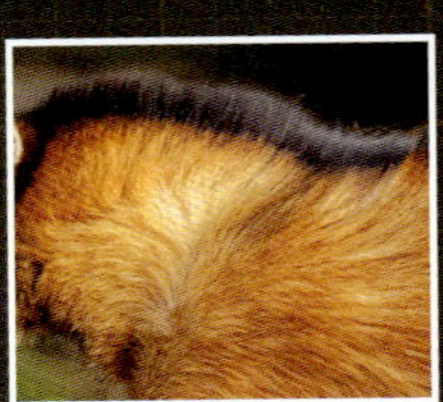

DARK MANE

Maned wolves use their dark manes as a **scare tactic**. They raise their shoulder and neck fur to appear larger and taller. This warns enemies to stay away.

Giant anteater tongues are 2 feet (0.6 meters) long. They stick their tongues deep into insect mounds. Their tongues are covered in sticky spit that traps prey.

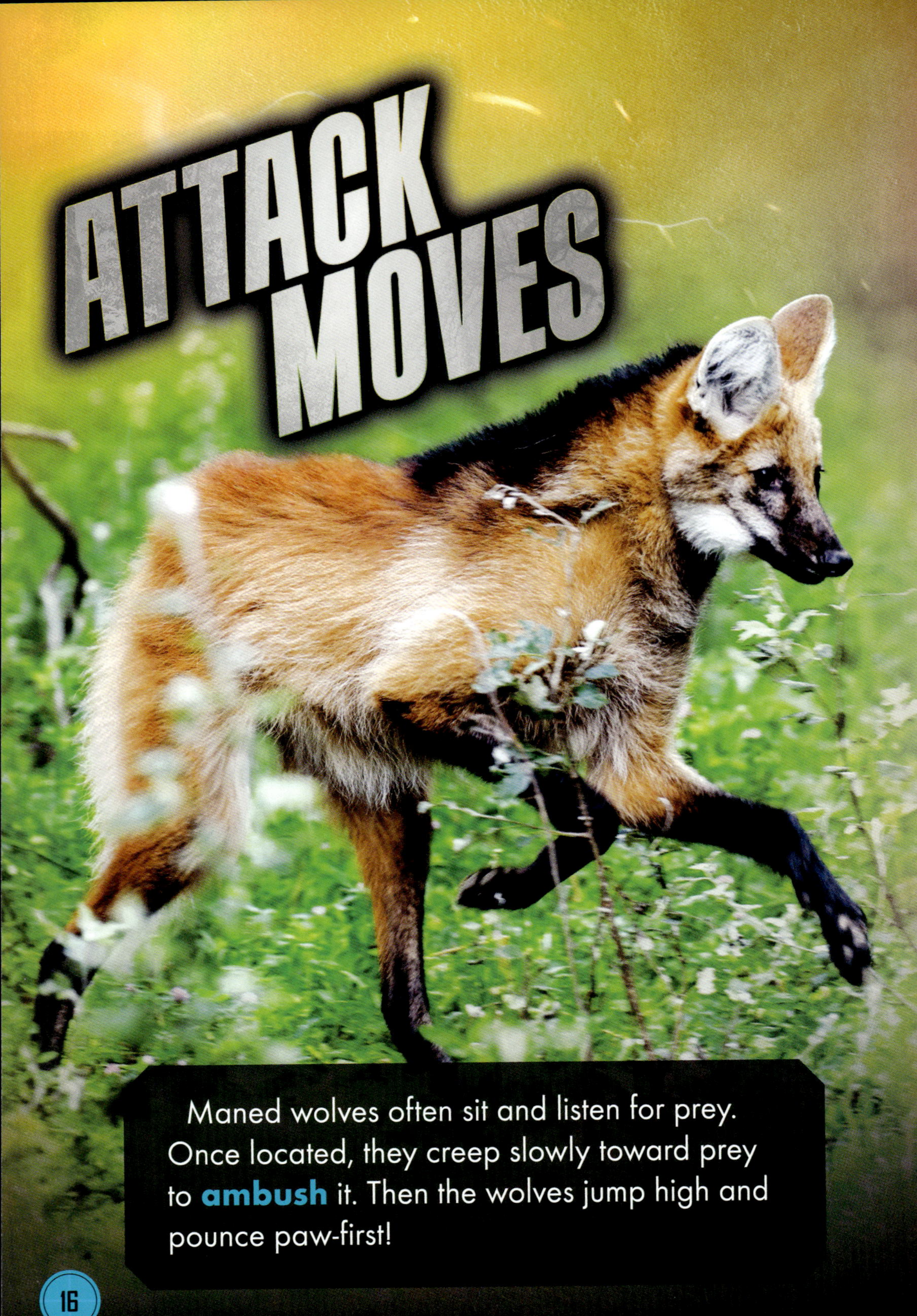

ATTACK MOVES

Maned wolves often sit and listen for prey. Once located, they creep slowly toward prey to **ambush** it. Then the wolves jump high and pounce paw-first!

Giant anteaters flick their tongues 150 times per minute when feeding. They crush food against the roofs of their mouths. Then they swallow it.

THOUSANDS OF INSECTS

One giant anteater can eat as many as 30,000 insects per day.

Maned wolves tap the ground to scare prey out of hiding. Then they chase it! They leap on prey to catch it. The wolves can also leap high to catch birds in midair!

DIGGING FOR FOOD

Maned wolves are known to dig out prey hidden underground.

Giant anteaters stand on their two back legs when fighting. Their large tails help them stay balanced. Then they use their long, sharp claws to cut and hurt enemies.

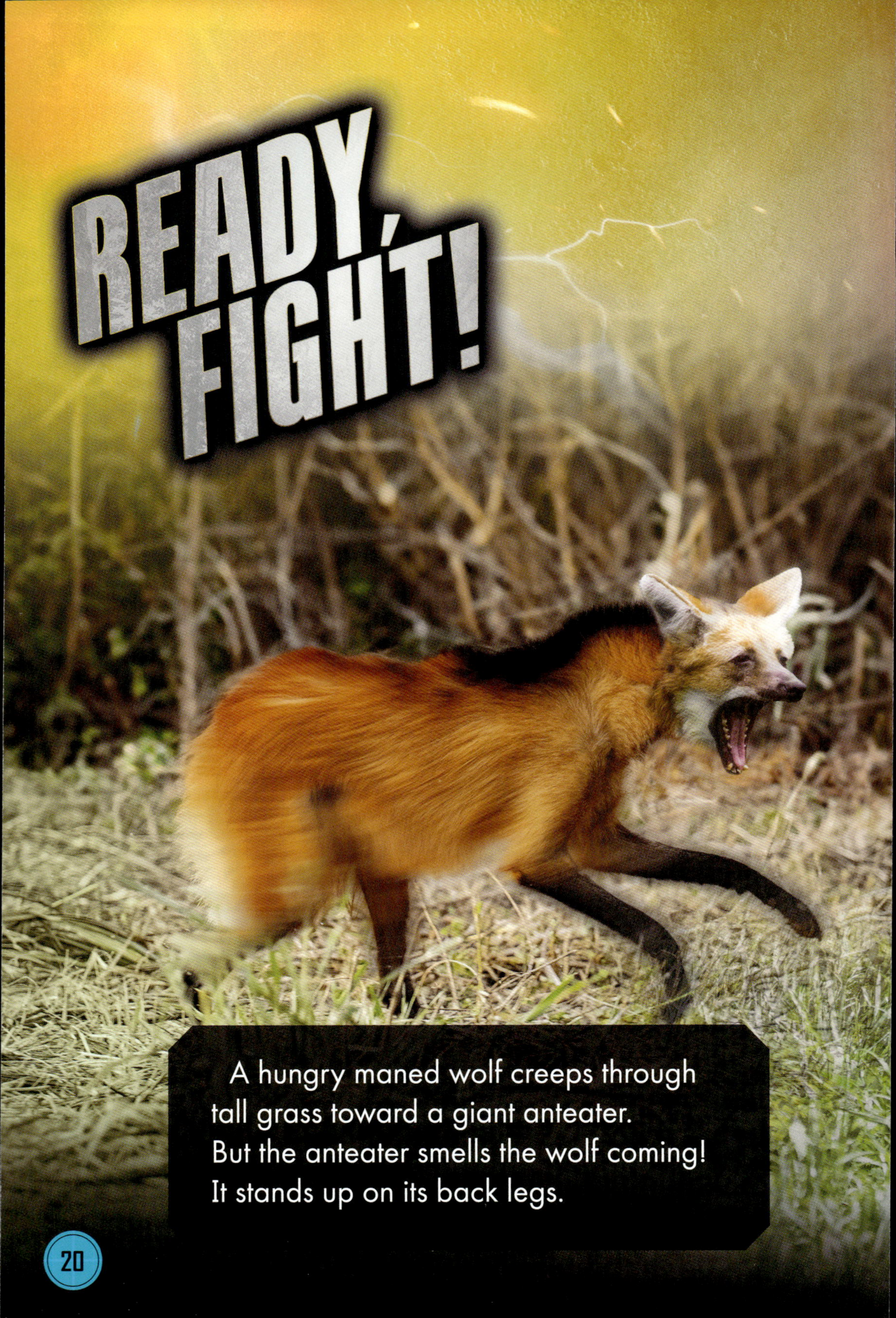

READY, FIGHT!

A hungry maned wolf creeps through tall grass toward a giant anteater. But the anteater smells the wolf coming! It stands up on its back legs.

The maned wolf pounces on the anteater. But the anteater slices the maned wolf with its claws. The anteater claws at the wolf until it is defeated. The giant anteater lives to see another day!

GLOSSARY

adapted—changed over a long period of time

ambush—to carry out a surprise attack

canines—dogs or a family that includes wolves, foxes, jackals, and dogs

habitats—the homes or areas where animals prefer to live

insect—a small animal with six legs and hard outer bodies; insect bodies are divided into three parts.

mammals—warm-blooded animals that have backbones and feed their young milk

predators—animals that hunt other animals for food

prey—animals that are hunted by other animals for food

scare tactic—a fighting strategy in which one animal tries to make itself appear as large or scary as possible in hopes of scaring the other off

snouts—the noses and mouths on some animals

wetlands—lands that are covered with low levels of water for most of the year

TO LEARN MORE

AT THE LIBRARY

Gish, Melissa. *Anteaters.* Mankato, Minn.: Creative Education and Creative Paperbacks, 2024.

Monroe, Alex. *The Dog Family.* Minneapolis, Minn.: Bellwether Media, 2026.

Watt, E. Melanie. *Giant Anteater.* New York, N.Y.: Lightbox Learning Inc., 2023.

ON THE WEB

FACTSURFER

Factsurfer.com gives you a safe, fun way to find more information.

1. Go to www.factsurfer.com
2. Enter "maned wolf vs. giant anteater" into the search box and click 🔍.
3. Select your book cover to see a list of related content.

INDEX

adapted, 4
ambush, 16
Central America, 8
claws, 5, 13, 19, 21
color, 7, 8
ears, 7, 10
fur, 7, 8
habitats, 4, 5, 6, 7, 8, 9
legs, 7, 12, 19, 20
mammals, 5, 8
manes, 14
noses, 11, 20
predators, 4, 12
prey, 4, 10, 12, 15, 16, 18
range, 6, 7, 8, 9
scare tactic, 14
size, 4, 6, 7, 8, 9, 10, 12, 13, 14, 15, 19
snouts, 8
South America, 4, 7, 8
speed, 12
tongues, 15, 17
weapons, 13, 14, 15

The images in this book are reproduced through the courtesy of: imageBROKER/ David & Micha Sheldon/ Alamy Stock Photo, front cover (maned wolf); Marcelo Morena, front cover (giant anteater); fotomaster, front cover (giant anteater arm); rudiernst, p. 4; Vinicius R. Souza, pp. 2 (maned wolf), 14 (dark mane), 20 (maned wolf), 22 (maned wolf); Bildagentur Zoonar GmbH, pp. 2 (maned wolf head), 20 (maned wolf head), 22 (maned wolf head); Pascale Gueret, pp. 3 (giant anteater), 21 (giant anteater), 23-24 (giant anteater); CheriAlguire, p. 5; Digital Dreams Studi, p. 6 (maned wolf vector); Octavio Campos Salles/ Alamy Stock Photo, pp. 6-7; Galyna Andrushko, pp. 8-9; Svetsol, p. 9 (anteater vector); Ger Bosma/ Alamy Stock Photo, p. 10; Alexandr Sanin/ Getty Images, p. 11; Tui De Roy/ Minden, p. 12; Kevin Carvalho, p. 13; Diego Grandi, pp. 14 (excellent hearing), 15 (powerful nose); Dennis Jacobsen, p. 14 (long legs); Luftaufnahme Bayern/ Getty Images, p. 14; Rob Jansen, p. 14 (background); dennisjacobsen, p. 15 (sharp front claws); GR92100, p. 15 (long tongue); David Pillow, p. 15; Janusz Pie kowski/ Alamy Stock Photo, p. 16; Jurgen and Christine Sohns/ Minden, p. 17; David & Micha Sheldon/ Getty Images, p. 18; Mark Newman/ Getty Images, p. 19.